A Cold Land

by Dawn McMillan

Harcourt
SCHOOL PUBLISHERS

Cover–8 ©Photolibrary.com.

Printed in the United States of America

ISBN 10: 0-15-349952-4
ISBN 13: 978-0-15-349952-4

Ordering Options
ISBN 10: 0-15-349936-2 (Grade 1 ELL Collection)
ISBN 13: 978-0-15-349936-4 (Grade 1 ELL Collection)
ISBN 10: 0-15-357182-9 (package of 5)
ISBN 13: 978-0-15-357182-4 (package of 5)

2 3 4 5 6 7 8 9 10   179   15 14 13 12 11 10 09 08 07

This is a cold land.

Look at the snow
and ice.

Small plants grow
here.

It is too cold for
trees to grow.

Animals live here.

This fox is white like
the snow.

Some people live
here, too!